Annabelle and Aiden
looked into a lake.
They saw their reflection
and did a double-take.

The wise owl watched
from up in his tree,
waiting for questions
about what they'd seen.

Annabelle said:
"Why do we look
the way that we do?
With hands and feet
in neat sets of two?

"What made my eyes?
And what made my nose?
And the shape of my body
from my head to my toes?"

"Finding these answers
will take far too much work.
Just say it was magic,"
Aiden said with a smirk.

2

The wise owl answered,
"Then how will you learn?
We live to discover,"
he said with concern.

"You'll be pleased to know
that the answer you seek
is quite magical itself.
So please take a seat.

"I'll tell you the story
how it all came to pass:
the structure of life
from the birds to the grass."

3

Once upon a time,
from far and near,
hung zillions of planets
for billions of years.

"There are at least 100-400 billion galaxies, each containing hundreds of billions of pla

4

" Humans live in less than % 0.000 000 000 000 000 015 of the universe's space for % 0.0007246 of its history-"

When in a little corner,
on a tiny blue dot,
deep under the ocean,
in a very special spot...

THE MOON WAS MUCH
CLOSER TO EARTH
(APPEARING LARGER) AND STILL
RETREATS AT ABOUT THE SAME
SPEED OUR FINGERNAILS GROW

An itty bitty thing
woke up anew,
and came alive.
I tell you, it's true!

6

PRECAMBRIAN PERIOD

heavily bombardment

The first living thing
that ever came to be!
It looked all around,
and what did it see?

A beautiful world of
earth, water, and stone.
There was so much to share,
but it was all alone.

The earth's rotation is still slowing - 500 million years ago, a day was 22 hours long.

OVER
3.6 BILLION
YRS AGO

Blue skies and mountains.
Oceans without end.
But to share this world,
it needed a friend.

7

So it pushed and it pushed
and it managed to create
a perfect copy of itself:
a new friend and mate.

And together they made
more friends to be 'round,
floating up through the oceans,
crawling down on the ground.

But when they copied themselves,
(though they tried best they could,)
some came out a bit different
than the others often would.

8

With slight random changes,
few were helpful, most, not.
Tiny mouths or teeny fins
or eyes as small as dots.

Those with helpful changes
could make babies of their own
a lot more than the others
who were more and more alone.

CAMBRIAN PERIOD
541 - 485.4 million yrs ago

Anomalocaris

Trilobites

sponges

9

So as (much) time went by,
the animals would change
into whatever sort of form
their environment arranged.

Corals and plants,
and sponges and spores.
Jellies and eels
and fishes galore!

Looking for more food
than they could find at hand,
they began their journey
from water onto land.

Some mouths became beaks
that could dig in the sand.
Some fins became legs
that could walk on the land.

Lizards and snakes
all crawled on the beach.
With mushrooms and plants
and flowers and bees.

Archaeopteris

Tiktaalik

Ichthyostega

380 - 360
million yrs
ago

11

Spiders and butterflies
all dancing around,
celebrating their trip
from water to ground.

12

Some joined in the dance,
but stayed close to the waters,
like lizards and seals,
frogs, turtles, and otters.

Some became dinosaurs,
then penguins and birds,
aside mice, rats, and wolves,
and small elephant herds.

Some primates became apes,
like the funny chimpanzee.
While others became people,
just like you and like me.

13

And we're all still evolving.
Into what, we can guess.
Can you imagine the ways
we all might change next?

"But how do we know?"
Aiden asked with much doubt
"That's my favorite question!
One we can't do without.

14

Well, besides all the fossils,
and our genes and DNA,
our body tells the story
with more clues than I can say.

WHALES EVOLVED FROM LAND MAMMALS

2 holes evolved from a land nose

There are many things Science does not yet know, such as exactly how life began, or how birds know their way South... Like evolution, atomic theory is not one of these things. Like evolution, atomic theory is an established fact. How? Thanks to today's information age, finding these answers have never been easier.

wrist and fingers

TADPOLES EVOLVED "HICCUPS" TO PUSH WATER ACROSS THEIR GILLS...
BUT DID THEY REALLY HAVE TO GIVE THEM TO US?!

HICCUP!

AND HAIR?
AND LUNGS?

Whales still have leg bones
from their time on the land.
People still have tail bones
you can feel with your hand!

(Try it!)

If you go back far enough, people, like most mammals, evolved from fish.

Human embryos still retain ancestral characteristics. They have (1) tails (which later get absorbed) (2) slits where fish grow gills (which later form our jaw/ear canal) (3) gonads in our chest like a fish (which later descend where it's cooler, "squishy") and (4) our nose (which later face", with eyes on our sides (which later squish together", resulting in the groove under our nose).

gill slits

tail

Before you kids were born, you grew
much like a fish still grows:
with eyes on your sides, which merged to make
that groove under your nose.

(touch it!)

Our primal ancestors would stand their fur on end (1) when scared/ threatened, to look bigger and more threatening, or (2) when cold, to create insulation. That's why we get goosebumps in those 2 situations, our hair standing on end. We have (now mostly useless) muscles around our ears, traces from our ancestors who's descendants still move their ears to locate sounds.

You had slits that turn to gills in fish,
but for you, they formed your jaw.
And a tail that snakes and chimps still use
to make sure they never fall.

Our wisdom teeth and goosebumps,
and the way we wiggle our ears,
are just a few of the countless clues
that tell us how we got here.

16

Every living thing,
people from every single race,
their dogs, cats, and flowers,
come from the same exact place.

你好

A young boy in Africa,
the grass, bugs and bees,
your teacher's pet parrot
who speaks Cantonese.

We are all related,
whether owl, boy, or girl.
Even you, me, and Aiden,
with the rest of the world.

Fishe

Protosomes

Fungi

Plants

Bacteria

Ingredients
of Life

Sulfur

Carbon

Hydrogen

Oxygen

Phosphorus

Nitrogen

All dogs came from wolves. All birds came from dinosaurs. All monkeys and humans came from earlier primates. And all of those, if you go back far enough, came from fish. Who also share an ancestor.

Reptiles

Mammals

Birds

Every animal, every single form of life, all share a common ancestor.

Primates

We all share the same story.
So what does this mean?
Just take a small look
at our family tree...

19

It reminds us to be kind,
and to treat each other well.
That we are all connected,
and together we must dwell.

Look again at that dot. That's here. That's home. That's us. On it everyone you love, everyone you know, everyone you ever heard of, every human being who ever was, lived out their lives. The Earth is the only home you've ever known.

"There is nowhere else, at least in the near future, to which our species could migrate. Visit, yes. Settle, not yet. Like it or not, for the moment the Earth is where we make our stand."

— Carl Sagan

This world belongs to all of us,
equally to share.
To hold hands together,
as we breathe the same air.

A NOTE TO (CURIOUS) PARENTS WHO WANT TO LEARN MORE: SO, IN SHORT, HOW DOES EVOLUTION ACTUALLY WORK? I EXPLAINED ON PAGES 8-10, BUT YOU WANT A BETTER IDEA. YOU NEED TO UNDERSTAND 2 THINGS. FIRST, GENETIC MUTATION. SEE, WHEN AN ANIMAL (LIKE, SAY, YOU) PRODUCES OFFSPRING (BABIES!), THE PARENT PASSES ON ITS GENES TO THE OFFSPRING, TO MAKE AN EXACT COPY OF ITSELF. OR TRIES TO. SEE, SOMETIMES THE DNA MAKES A MISTAKE. IT MESSES UP. AND, INSTEAD OF MAKING A PERFECT, EXACT COPY OF ITSELF IN YOUR BABY, IT MAKES A COPY THAT IS A BIT DIFFERENT. WITH TINY, RANDOM CHANGES. YOUR KIDS DON'T ALL HAVE THE SAME EXACT HAIR, SKIN, OR EYE COLOR AS YOU, DO THEY? A GENETIC MUTATION OR VARIATION HAS OCCURRED. NOW, WE COME TO THE SECOND THING YOU HAVE TO UNDERSTAND: ENVIRONMENTAL FILTRATION (OR NATURAL SELECTION). OVER TIME (OKAY, LOTS AND LOTS OF TIME,) THE (VERY, VERY RARE AND FEW) ANIMALS WITH THE RANDOM GENETIC MUTATIONS THAT JUST SO HAPPEN TO HELP THEM SURVIVE IN THEIR ENVIRONMENT (SUCH AS, BY HAVING WHITE CAMOUFLAGING FUR IN THE ARCTIC, WEBBED FEET ON SAND OR WATER, OR EYES AT THE TOP OF THEIR FACE FOR A BETTER VIEW) WERE ABLE TO SURVIVE LONGER, AND THUS, AS WOULD MAKE SENSE, HAD (MORE OF) AN OPPORTUNITY TO CREATE MORE OFFSPRING. SEE, OUR ENVIRONMENT WORKS AS A FILTER TO WEED OUT THE BAD MODELS. OUR ENVIRONMENT WASN'T MADE FOR US, BUT RATHER, IT'S THE OTHER WAY AROUND. OUR BODY IS STRUCTURED THE WAY IT IS BECAUSE ALL THE OTHER RANDOMLY-GENERATED DESIGNS (WHICH, BY THE WAY, WERE THE VAST MAJORITY OF DESIGNS GENERATED) DIDN'T MAKE IT. THEY WERE SHODDY AND INEFFECTIVE. THEY WEREN'T HELPFUL. (IF THIS IS ALL RANDOM, WHY WOULD THEY BE? THEY WERE MISTAKES!) WE ARE THE GENETIC MUTATIONS THAT MADE IT THROUGH! OUR BODY IS STRUCTURED THE WAY IT IS BECAUSE IT HAS TO BE, TO EXIST. WE'RE THE TINY MINORITY WHO MADE IT THUS FAR. WE'RE THE SURVIVORS! THE SHAPE OF OUR BODY IS LIKE THE SHAPE OF WATER IN A CONTAINER: IT HAS TO TAKE THAT SHAPE TO CONFORM TO ITS SURROUNDINGS. WE ARE THE MALLEABLE CLAY THAT, AFTER GETTING PRESSED THROUGH A STAR-SHAPED HOLE (AND LEAVING BEHIND MOST OF ITSELF), LOOKS BACK, SEES THE STAR SHAPE ITS BODY HAS BECOME, AND EXCLAIMS, "HOW PERFECT THAT HOLE'S SHAPE IS FOR ME - MY BODY FITS PERFECTLY!" NO. YOUR BODY NEVER LOOKED LIKE THAT UNTIL IT WENT THROUGH THAT HOLE. IT WAS FORCED INTO THAT SHAPE BY THAT HOLE. THERE WERE OTHER PARTS OF YOU - THEY JUST DIDN'T MAKE IT THROUGH. AND IF THE HOLE LOOKED ANY DIFFERENT, SO WOULD YOU (AND YOU'D BE SAYING THE SAME THING!) I KNOW, THIS IS HARD TO CONCEIVE, BECAUSE WE ARE BORN TO AWAKE TO SEE THE FINISHED PRODUCT, AFTER BILLIONS OF YEARS OF REFINEMENT. AND AFTER ALL THAT FILTRATION, TODAY, WE ONLY SEE OURSELVES. WE DON'T SEE THE FAILED DESIGNS. THE OVER-99.99% OF BOTCHED DESIGNS THAT OCCURRED. THEY'VE BEEN NATURALLY DISCARDED. THEY FAILED. THERE WAS GENETIC MUTATION (AND STILL IS) BUT THE ENVIRONMENT FILTERED THEM OUT (AND STILL DOES.) LEAVING US. (FEEL LUCKY?) FOR ANY INTENT TO CREATE OUR SPECIES OF MODERN HUMAN, THIS METHOD WOULD HAVE TO BE THE MOST PAINSTAKINGLY ONEROUS, WASTEFUL, ROUNDABOUT WAY TO GET THERE. THE VAST MAJORITY OF THE TIME LIFE EXISTED ON EARTH, IT EXISTED AS TINY BACTERIA AND SINGLE (AND FAR LATER, MULTI) CELLULAR LIFE, FLOATING AROUND MURKY WATERS. FOR ABOUT 90% OF LIFE'S HISTORY IT TOOK BILLIONS OF YEARS FOR A COUPLE OF THOSE CELLS TO DEVELOP TINY EYES, AND EVENTUALLY, TINY HOLES TO DIGEST FOOD THAT WOULD LATER BE MOUTHS, AND WELL, YOU GET THE IDEA. AND SINCE, OVER 99% OF SPECIES HAVE GONE EXTINCT. BILLIONS OF YEARS LATER, WE JUST SHOWED UP. ONLY 100,000 YEARS AGO. FEELS LIKE YESTERDAY, HUH? GENETIC MUTATION AND ENVIRONMENTAL FILTRATION, BABY. SING IT! WHY? EVOLUTION IS THE CORNERSTONE OF BIOLOGY. SO MUCH WE DO RESTS UPON OUR KNOWLEDGE OF IT: FROM THE WAY WE GROW CROPS TO HOW WE MAKE MEDICINE. IT ANSWERS HUNDREDS OF QUESTIONS. HOW DO ANTIBIOTICS WORK? WHERE DID DOGS COME FROM? WHAT'S OUR APPENDIX FOR? OR OUR WISDOM TEETH? HOW DID LAND MAMMALS GET TO AUSTRALIA? (KANGAROOS CAN'T JUMP THAT FAR). WITHOUT THE THEORY OF EVOLUTION, EVERYTHING FALLS APART. NOTHING WOULD MAKE SENSE. UNDERSTANDING HOW AND WHY WE EVOLVED CERTAIN BODY PARTS, LET ALONE CERTAIN PSYCHOLOGICAL TENDENCIES OR A MORAL SENSE, IS FASCINATING. BUT FOR NOW, WE CAN ENJOY AND CELEBRATE OUR KINSHIP WITH ALL EARTHLY LIFE: WE ALL EVOLVED FROM THE SAME ANCESTOR. SCIENCE REMINDS US THAT DESPITE THE NATIONALIST, RELIGIOUS, RACIAL, OR POLITICAL DIVIDES WE INSIST ON CATEGORIZING OURSELVES BY, WHEN IT COMES DOWN TO IT, THEY'RE ARBITRARY. RACE IS A RELATIVELY RECENT ANOMALY. AND OTHER CATEGORIES, EVEN MORESO. FROM THE BEGINNING, WE'VE MADE THIS JOURNEY TOGETHER. WE'RE ALL RELATIVES ON THE SAME ROCK, HURTLING THROUGH SPACE TOGETHER, DESTINED TO THE SAME FATE. WE HAVE TO WORK TOGETHER, BECAUSE WE ARE TOGETHER. AND IN OUR WORLD TODAY, SUCH A FACT MAY NOT BE THE WORST LESSON TO TELL. BESIDES, IT'D SURE MAKE FOR A PRETTY GREAT CHILDREN'S BOOK. -J.R.BECKER

CPSIA information can be obtained
at www.ICGtesting.com
Printed in the USA
BVHW022047190822
644978BV00010B/31